A BRIEF OUTLINE OF
RELIGIOUS
HISTORY
AND THE GROWING DANGER AHEAD

MM

Order this book online at www.trafford.com
or email orders@trafford.com

Most Trafford titles are also available at major online book retailers.

Printed in the United States of America.

ISBN: 978-1-4907-3295-4 (sc)
ISBN: 978-1-4907-3296-1 (hc)
ISBN: 978-1-4907-3297-8 (e)

Library of Congress Control Number: 2014906253

Trafford rev. 04/02/2014

 www.trafford.com

North America & international
toll-free: 1 888 232 4444 (USA & Canada)
fax: 812 355 4082

Contents

FOREWORD

THIS PAPER WAS WRITTEN BECAUSE the author (MM) believes a great threat to world peace is imminent. The subjects raised in leading to, and in support of, this belief are intentionally brief and included only to lead to the conclusion. There are volumes written on each subject and available to anyone with a further interest. The potential solution to the threat will be extremely difficult to accomplish for many reasons but must be attempted.

1

Religions Today

WHAT IS THOUGHT TO BE the first known "religion" dates from 3,000 BC in Mesopotamia. Writings in cuneiform on clay tablets suggest that the leader of the early cities was not only considered a king but was worshiped as a deity. It is believed that before this time ancient peoples named the sun, moon and the five planets they could see (Mercury, Venus, Mars, Jupiter and Saturn) as their various gods.

Today there are hundreds of religions being practiced around the world. The four largest are Christianity, Hinduism, Islam and Judaism. Other long established major world religions, each with over 3 million followers, include: Baha'i Faith, Buddhism, Confucianism, Jainism, Shinto, Sikhism, Taoism and Vodun (Voodoo). There are many more smaller religions with a well-defined belief in deity, humanity and the rest of the universe. These include the following:

Caodaism	Gypsies	Rom, Roma, Romani
Damanhur Community	Hare Krishna-Iskcon	Satanism
Deism	IFA	Scientology
Druse	Lukumi	Unitarian-Universalism
Eckankar	Macumba	Yazdanism
Gnosticism	Muwahhidun	Zoroastrianism

Types of pagan religions still practiced today include: Asatru, Druidism, Goddess Worship, Wicca and Witchcraft.

Of the hundreds of religions known today all but one has learned to live in peace and for the most part let others practice their beliefs without fear as they see fit. Many religions actively seek new members to their beliefs. Most people reading this will have had the Seventh-day Adventists knock on their door. The Christian bible says in Matthew 28: 19: Go ye and make disciples of all nations. This has always been done in peace (with the exception of the Spanish and others in the new world). On the other hand in Islamic thought, Dar al-Islam means total submission to Allah, and Dar al-Hard means war against the rest of the world. Only one religion, as far as I know, condones, even urges, the killing of anyone who does not believe as they do and refuses to convert to their religion.

An interesting thought is that each of us is what we are by pure chance. If your god had willed it, or the stork had the wrong address, each of us could be of a different faith. Think about this, if you were born in the U.S. you most certainly would be Christians; in India: Hindu; in the Far East: Buddhist; in Iran: Muslim: in Europe: secular. Had you been born in another culture and provided an education, how would you view other religions?

There are many smaller religions around the world including a few in which the followers have committed suicide in their belief of some eternal afterlife. In 1978, 912 people died in Jonestown, Guyana, after Peoples Temple cult leader Jim Jones persuaded most followers to kill themselves by drinking cyanide-laced punch. Others were shot to death or forcibly poisoned.

It is hard to understand how in this modern civilized world with mass information flow (news media, internet, global cell phones and world-wide travel) that we still have so many religions outside the mainstream. But then I think about what some of the most advanced civilizations of the past practiced and I wonder if everything we believe today will be just as strange a few thousand years from now.

2
Major Religions/Myths of the Past

FOR THOUSANDS OF YEARS THE ancient Egyptians, considered by many to be the most advanced civilization of their time, worshipped some 2000 gods. They had a god for almost every aspect of life. Some gods were perceived as symbols but many more were in the form of animals and others as part animal and part human. They also believed that Atum, their main god, created everything including himself.

Following is a list of gods, symbols and animals considered major Egyptian gods:

God of	Name	Appearance	Symbol	Nature
Sun	Ra	head of falcon and sun disk	White crown	Cobra
Music	Hathor	horns of cow and sun disk	Red crown	Falcon
Destruction	Sekhmet	head of lion	Eye of Horus	Ibis
Sky	Nut	blue with golden stars	Feather of Ma'at	Scarab
Earth	Geb	colour of plants and Nile mud	Ankh	beetle
Dead	Osiris	dressed in white with crook and flail	Sceptre of Seth	Moon
			Sun disk	Ram
Desert	Seth	animal head with long curved snout	Boat of Ra	Ammonite
Pharoah	Horus	head of hawk and crown of Egypt	Crook and flail	
			Scarab	
Magic	Isis	throne on head or holding baby	**Monsters**	
Wisdom	Thoth	head of ibis	Ammit the destroyer	
Embalming	Anubis	head of jackal	Apep the snake	
Justice	Ma'at	feather in her hair		
Creation	Amun	crowned with feathers		
Cats	Bastet	head of cat		

About 1350 BC Akhenaten became pharaoh of Egypt at a time when the god Amon held the highest place among the many gods. He soon discarded Amon and turned his belief to another deity called Aten. Akhenaten believed Aten was the only god except Re, the sun god. He discarded the whole religious structure which put thousands of priests out of work and banned the worship of Amon. Akhenaten died in the eighteenth year of his reign and soon after his belief in Aten was overturned.

Tutankhamen, the 9-year-old son of Akhenaten, became the next pharaoh. Since he was a child, it is believed his mother and influential priests actually ruled and turned the country back to the old gods and reinstated the priests. Everything connected with Akhenaten was soon destroyed or demolished and his mummy has never been found.

The ancient Greek mankind, trying to explain certain metaphysical phenomena and anxieties, invented amazing myths concerning the Cosmogony (the creation of the World) and the Theogony (the birth of the Gods). Thus, the ancient Greek people created their own splendid yet human-like world of gods, justifying the various abstract significances like Love, Birth or Death.

The origins of the gods or ancient Greek religion are described in the *Theogony,* the famous poem of the Greek writer Hesiod (around 700 BC) and the Library of Apollodorus.

The creation of the gods needs to be divided into four parts:

1. The Coming into Existence of Chaos

First there was Chaos, a rough unordered mass of things, also considered as a void. Chaos was followed by Gaea (Earth) and Eros (Desire), who came to cancel every logical thought or act. Gaea then brought Uranus (the Heaven), Pontus (the Sea) and the Mountains to the world

2. The Castration of Uranus

Uranus' task was to surround and cover Gaea with his starry coat, however, it very soon came to a union between Uranus and Gaea and they became the first divine couple in the world

Gaea bore Uranus twelve Titans and furthermore three Cyclops, Brontes, Steropes and heady Arges, and three Hecatonchires (Hundred-Handed creatures).

Uranus was fearful of his children overthrowing him, so he pushed his children back one by one into the womb of Gaea. His wife Gaea was in deep grief and sorrow over the loss of her own children, so in the end she handed a sickle to her son Cronus, the youngest of the Titans, in order to castrate his father.

Cronus castrated his father while he was sleeping; the blood from Uranus was collected by Mother Earth Gaea and she produced Erinyes (Furies), Giants and Melian nymphs. Cronus then threw his father's genitals into the sea, around which foams developed, that started in Kythera and then slowly made their way to the island of Paphos. In Paphos, the foams transformed into Aphrodite, the Olympian goddess of Love and Beauty.

3. Zeus' Escape from the Threat of Cronus

Soon afterwards, Cronus rescues his brothers and sisters and shares the World (Cosmos) with them. He then marries Rhea and together they created children who later on would become the Olympian gods. But Cronus developed the same fear as his father so he started to swallow his own children as well.

Rhea was highly discomforted so, on her attempt to save her youngest child, Zeus, she deceived Cronus by giving him a huge stone to swallow. To protect her son afterwards, Rhea then sent Zeus to Crete.

4. The Victorious Battle of the Olympian Gods against the Titans (Titanomachy)

Zeus grew up in Crete, fed by the goat Amaltheia and was taken good care of by the Nymphs. When he reached manhood, as prophesied, Zeus rescued his five elder brothers and sisters and then made war on his father and the Titans, also known as "Titanomachy". In this battle, Zeus succeeded in overthrowing Cronus, casting him and the other titans into the depths of the Underworld. A huge battle with the Giants followed, where the Olympian Gods excelled and then time had come for the Olympian gods to rule the world.

First Greek Gods

- Theogony
- Chaos
- The Titans

The Olympian Gods

- Aphrodite
- Apollo
- Ares
- Artemis
- Athena
- Demeter
- Dionysus
- Hades
- Hephaestus
- Hera
- Hermes
- Hestia
- Poseidon
- Zeus

Semi-Gods and Spirits

- Furies (Erinyes)
- Graces (Charities)
- Fates (Moirae)
- Muses
- Nymphs
- Sirens

Monsters & Creatures

- Centaurs
- Cyclopes
- Giants
- Satyrs

Greek Heroes

- Achilles
- Agamemnon
- Heracles
- Jason & the Argonauts
- Odysseus
- Theseus

The Roman gods were from a strange mixture of influences. Before Rome became a big city, the area around it, called Latium, was settled by superstitious villagers, the Latins, who believed in many gods and spirits. As Rome grew into a city and began to become more powerful, it came into contact with the Greeks who had a complex Pantheon of their own. It seems that the Roman gods were a mix of those two main influences: Latin and Greek. In many cases the Romans found there were a Latin and a Greek god for one and the same thing. They tended to take the two and make them one. So, for example, Vulcan was the old Latin god of fire. But the

Greeks had a god called Hephaistos who was very similar. So the Romans just mixed the two together and made them one. Paintings or statues of Vulcan generally showed him as a blacksmith, like the Greek Hephaistos, but his name still was the Latin Vulcan.

The Romans believed in many different gods and goddesses. For everything imaginable they had a god or goddess in charge. Mars for example was the god of war. This meant he was good at fighting and it meant that he had most of the soldiers at heart. A Roman soldier would hence most likely pray to Mars for strength in battle. Minerva was the goddess of wisdom, intelligence and learning, but not many soldiers would ask her for help. Perhaps a schoolboy would ask her to help him learn his grammar or understand his math better. Or the emperor would ask her to give him wisdom so that he might rule the country wisely. So the Romans indeed had hundreds of different gods. This entire collection of all their gods was called the Pantheon.

In Roman religion every household had its own personal spirits which protected it. The Lares were the spirits of the family's ancestors. The Penates were kind spirits who guarded the larder. Little figurines of these spirits were kept in a small household shrine called the lararium. The spirits would be worshipped by the family on special days. Bits of food or wine might be sacrificed to them.

With the vast size of the empire there were, of course, many new gods from distant civilizations which the Romans learned about. Romans didn't tend to think that only their gods were the right ones. If they heard of other peoples' gods they would think that these were real gods who watched over other parts of the world and whom they had simply not yet heard about. And, so as they learned about these new gods, new temples were built to these new arrivals in the Roman pantheon.

In the year 312 AD something very important happened, something which would change Roman religion forever. The emperor Constantine the Great said he had received a sign from the god of the Christians in a dream the night before he had an important battle. Emperor Constantine won this battle and thereafter showed his gratitude to the Christian god by turning his entire empire over to this new religion.

Some Roman Gods:

Jupiter—King of the Gods	Minerva—Goddess of Wisdom
Juno—Queen of the Gods	Ceres—The Earth Goddess
Neptune—God of the Sea	Proserpine—Goddess of the Underworld
Pluto—God of Death	Vulcan—The Smith God
Apollo—God of the Sun	Bacchus—God of Wine
Diana—Goddess of the Moon	Saturn—God of Time
Mars—God of War	Vesta—Goddess of the Home
Venus—Goddess of Love	Janus—God of Doors
Cupid—God of Love	Uranus and Gaia—Parents of Saturn
Mercury—Messenger of the Gods	Maia—Goddess of Growth

Monsters:

Cerberus—Dog of the Underworld
Gorgon—Turns you to stone

The Maya, who like the Aztec and Inca who came to power later, believed in cyclical nature of time. Ancient objects known as codices, suggest they practiced human sacrifice. However, it is known that they believed the cosmos had 3 major planes: the earth, the underworld beneath and the heavens above. The rain god Chaac resided in caves and natural wells called cenotes. Mayan farmers today still appeal to Chaac for rain. Other gods included Ixchel, the goddess of fertility, and a mythic Maya lord of death.

3

Evolution vs Creation

THE MODERN UNDERSTANDING OF EVOLUTION began with the 1859 publication of Charles Darwin's *"The Origin of Species."* Gregor Mendel's work with plants helped to explain the hereditary patterns of genetics. Darwin's theory of evolution by natural selection is one of the best substantiated theories in the history of science, supported by evidence from a wide variety of scientific disciplines, including paleontology, geology, genetics and developmental biology.

A recent article in the New York Times stated that 67% of Democrats and 43% of Republicans believe in evolution. I could not find any informed information on % of worldwide belief in evolution but tend to think it would be quite high among modern educated people.

The Vatican also sought to show that it isn't opposed to science and evolutionary theory, hosting a conference on Charles Darwin and trying to debunk the idea that it embraces creationism or intelligent design. Some of the world's top biologists, paleontologists and molecular geneticists joined theologians and philosophers for the five-day seminar marking the 150th anniversary of Darwin's *"The Origin of Species."*

Cardinal William Levada, head of the Vatican's congregation for the doctrine of the faith, said the Catholic Church doesn't stand in the way of scientific realities like evolution, saying there was a "wide spectrum of room" for belief in both the scientific basis for evolution and faith in

God the creator. He added that however creation has come about and evolved, ultimately God is the creator of all things. Creationism refers to the belief that the universe and everything in it were created by a god. It refers to a supernatural deity or force that intervenes, or has intervened, directly in the physical world. Creationism is the belief in the literal interpretation of the account of the creation of the universe and of all living things related in the bible.

The Creation Museum is a museum that presents an account of the origins of the universe, life, mankind, and man's early history according to a literal, young earth creationist perspective of the Book of Genesis in the bible. The museum was originally marketed as the Creation Museum and Family Discovery Center. It opened on May 28, 2007, as Creation Museum. The museum is located north-northeast of Petersburg, Kentucky, roughly 12 miles from the Cincinnati/ Northern Kentucky International Airport on 49 acres of land. The Answers in Genesis main offices are attached to the museum. The facility's stated mission is to "exalt Jesus Christ as Creator, Redeemer and Sustainer," to "equip Christians to better evangelize the lost" and "to challenge visitors to receive Jesus Christ as Savior and Lord."

The museum has been criticized as promoting "fallacy over fact" and attempting to advance the tenets of a particular religious view while rejecting, overlooking and misconstruing scientific knowledge. The museum has received criticism from the scientific community, several groups of educators, Christian groups opposed to young earth creationism and in the press.

Its exhibits reject universal common descent and biological evolution, and assert that the Earth and all of its life forms were created 6,000 years ago over a six-day period. In contrast to the scientific consensus, exhibits promote young earth creationist claims, including the idea that humans and dinosaurs once coexisted, and that dinosaurs were on Noah's Ark. Scientific evidence supports the conclusions that the earth is approximately 4.5 billion years old, and that the dinosaurs became extinct 65.5 million years before human beings arose.

In 2009 the Creation Museum added a one room display devoted to Charles Darwin. The display argues that natural selection—Darwin's explanation how new species develop because of new traits or new environments—can coexist with the creationist assertion that all living things were created by God just a few thousand years ago.

Educators criticizing the museum include the National Center for Science Education. The NCSE collected over 800 signatures from scientists in the three states closest to the museum (Kentucky, Indiana and Ohio) on the following statement: "We, the undersigned scientists at universities and colleges in Kentucky, Ohio and Indiana, are concerned about scientifically inaccurate materials at the Answers in Genesis museum. Students who accept this material as scientifically valid are unlikely to succeed in science courses at the college level. These students will need remedial instruction in the nature of science, as well as in the specific areas of science misrepresented by Answers in Genesis."

4

Pascal's Wager—To Believe or Not

BLAISE PASCAL (1623-1662), FRENCH PHILOSOPHER, scientist, mathematician and probability theorist, offers a pragmatic reason for believing in God—even under the assumption that God's existence is unlikely, the potential benefits of believing are so vast as to make betting on theism rational.

	God Exists	God Does Not Exist
Wager For God	Gain All	Status Quo
Wager Against God	Misery	Status Quo

Or

	God Exists	God Does Not Exist
You Believe In God	Infinite Reward	+
You Do Not Believe In God	Infinite Punishment	-

There are two kinds of arguments for theism. Traditional, epistemic arguments hold that God exists; examples include arguments from cosmology, design, ontology and experience. Modern, pragmatic arguments hold that, regardless of whether God exists, believing in God is good for us, or is the right thing to do; examples include the 1896 William James' "The Will to Believe."

MM

Critics in turn have raised a number of now-classic challenges. According to intellectualism, deliberately choosing which beliefs to hold is practically impossible. Intellectualism, however, appears to be not only questionable but irrelevant. According to the many-gods objection, Pascal's wager begs the question and hence is irrational. It assumes that if God exists then God must take a rather specific form, which few open-minded agnostics would accept. Pascalians reply by invoking the notion of a genuine option (which is not defined), by devising run-off decision theory (which is not justified), by claiming that Pascal was understandably unaware of other cultures (which is not true) and by appealing to generic theism (which does not solve the problem).

Some Pascalians, while acknowledging that the Wager might be unsound for today's multi-culturally sophisticated audience, maintain that the Wager is sound relative to Pascal and his peers in the 1600s, when Catholicism, and agnosticism were the only possibilities (Rescher 1985,). But the Crusades in the 1100s taught the French of Islam, the Renaissance in the 1400s taught the French of Greco-Roman paganism, the discoveries of the 1500s taught the French of new-world paganism, and several wars of religion taught the French of Protestantism. To claim that the educated French of the 1600s rightfully rejected alien beliefs without consideration appears to endorse rank prejudice.

Pascal's compatriot Denis Diderot replied to the wager "that an ayatollah or imam could just as well reason the same way." His point is that decision theory cannot decide among the various religions practiced in the world; it gives no warrant for believing in Pascal's Catholicism, or even in a generic Judeo-Christianity. A more complete matrix must consider at least the following possibilities.

	Yahweh Exists	Allah Exists
You Worship Yahweh	Infinite Reward	Infinite Punishment
You Worship Allah	Infinite Punishment	Infinite Reward

When thinking about today's religions, it is difficult to believe they are all right—but reasonable to believe they could all be wrong.

A book by the legendary skeptic Martin Gardner suggested that perhaps there was a singular god ruling the universe and some potential for life after death. Carl Sagan, who had admired Gardner for many years, wrote to him: "The only reason for this position that I can find is that it feels good . . . how could you, of all people, advocate a position because it's emotionally satisfying rather than demand rigorous standards of evidence."

Gardner responded: "I not only think there is no proof of God or an afterlife. I think you have all the best arguments. Where we differ is over whether the leap of faith can be justified in spite of a total lack of evidence."

5

Science—Religion—Myth
(Our Place In The Universe)

FOR THOUSANDS OF YEARS PEOPLE believed the earth was flat and the center of the universe. Greek astronomy first proved the earth was spherical, but it was Copernicus in 1543 who published *"De Revolutionibus Orbium Coelectium Libri VI,"* six books on "the revolutions of the heavenly bodies" provided the proof. In addition, the works of Kepler, Galileo and Newton in the 17th century would forever do away with the concept of a flat earth and of the earth being the center of the universe.

As late as 1633 the Roman Catholic Church condemned Galileo for writing that the earth revolves around the sun. The church declared: the doctrine that the earth is neither the center of the universe nor immovable, but moves even with a daily rotation, is absurd and both psychologically and theologically false, and at least an error of faith.

It wasn't until the mid-1800's that the church allowed Catholics to read Galileo's works without punishment and until 1992 that Pope John Paul II admitted the church was wrong.

Today we know our earth is nothing more than a tiny dot in an obscure planetary system located in an outer ring of an average galaxy among an inconceivable number of galaxies all speeding apart into endless space. Our galaxy alone, the Milky Way, is estimated to be 100,000 light years across. Since light travels at 186,000 miles/second, the Milky Way may be over 5 quadrillion miles wide. Within our galaxy the distance between the closest Sun (Alpha Centauri) to our sun is about 25 trillion miles.

Ann Druyan (Carl Sagan—*Pale Blue Dot*) suggests an experiment. Think of our earth as this tiny dot in the universe and concentrate on it for any length of time. Then try to convince yourself that God created the whole universe for one of the 10 million or so species of life that inhabit this speck of dust. Now take it a step further. Imagine that everything was made just for a single shade of that species, or gender, or ethnic or religious subdivision. If this doesn't strike you as unlikely, pick another dot. Imagine it to be inhabited by a different form of intelligent life. They, too, cherish the notion of a god who has created everything for their benefit. How seriously do you take their claim?

Religion and myth have nothing in common with science. Joseph Campbell in *"The Inner Reaches of Outer Space"* defines the problem as follows: from the point of view of any orthodoxy, myth might be defined simply as "other people's religion," to which an equivalent definition of religion would be "misunderstood mythology." The misunderstanding consisting in the interpretation of mythic metaphors as references to hard fact: the virgin birth, for example, as a biological anomaly, or the Promised Land as a portion of the near east to be claimed and settled by a people chosen of god. The term "god" here to be understood as denoting an actual, though invisible, masculine personality, who created the universe and is now resident in an invisible, though actual, heaven to which the "justified" will go when they die to be joined at the end of time by their resurrected bodies. "What, in the name of reason or truth, is a modern mind to make of such evident nonsense?"

I believe it possible that great scientific discoveries within the next century will result in a new understanding of our role in the universe and the role of religion in our lives.

Think of how the invention of the internal combustion engine which led to the automobile and airplane changed our methods of transportation, or the invention of the telephone in 1876 that enabled people to speak to others over long distances, and the cell phone, which has changed the way people communicate around the world. Possibly the most important invention of the 20th century, the computer, has impacted almost every aspect of our lives. The rapid increase in the speed and power of the computer has been responsible for advances in every field you can imagine.

The rate of new scientific discoveries, new inventions, advances in medicine and the unraveling of DNA has been unprecedented and there doesn't seem to be any reason for it to slow down or stop.

A way to think about the expansion of knowledge and the realization that there is so much that we don't know or understand can be illustrated as follows:

Every bit of your knowledge is inside an inflatable balloon and everything you don't know is represented by the outer surface of your balloon. The more knowledge you gain, the bigger the balloon becomes and at the same time the surface area becomes larger. The more you know the more you don't know.

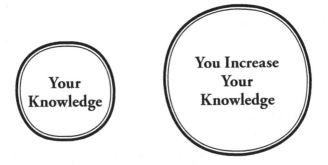

6

Separation of Church and State

ROGER WILLIAMS (1603-1683) WAS AN English protestant, theologian, statesman, author and an early proponent of religious freedom and the separation of church and state.

Although he took holy orders in the Church of England, he had become a puritan at Cambridge, forfeiting any chance at a place of preferment in the Anglican Church. Williams was privy to the plans of the puritan leaders to migrate to the new world, and he decided he could not remain in England under Archbishop William Laud's rigorous (and high church) administration. He regarded the Church of England to be corrupt and false, and by the time he and his wife sailed to the new world in 1630, he had arrived at the separatist position.

As a separatist he had concluded that it was necessary to completely separate from the Church of England to establish a new church for the true and pure worship of God. In 1636 Williams and a number of followers established a settlement calling it "Providence." He said that his settlement was to be a haven for those "distressed of conscience" and it soon attracted quite a collection of otherwise-minded individuals. Thus, Williams had founded the first place in modern history where citizenship and religion were separated, a place where there was religious liberty and separation of church and state.

Williams believed that the moral principles found in the scriptures ought to inform the civil magistrates, but he observed that well-ordered, just and civil magistrates existed where Christianity was not present. All governments were required to maintain civil order and justice, but none had a warrant to promote any religion.

"Separation of church and state" (sometimes "wall of separation between church and state") is a phrase used by Thomas Jefferson and others expressing an understanding of the intent and function of the Establishment Clause and Free Exercise Clause of the First Amendment to the Constitution of the United States.

The First Amendment to the United States Constitution provides that "Congress shall make no law respecting an establishment of religion, or prohibiting the free exercise thereof . . ." and Article VI specifies that "no religious Test shall ever be required as a Qualification to any Office or public Trust under the United States." The modern concept of a wholly secular government is sometimes credited to the writings of English philosopher John Locke, but the phrase "separation of church and state" in this context is generally traced to a January 1, 1802 letter by Thomas Jefferson, addressed to the Danbury Baptist Association in Connecticut and published in a Massachusetts newspaper.

Jefferson's metaphor of a wall of separation has been cited repeatedly by the U.S. Supreme Court.

In *Reynolds v. United States* (1879) the Court wrote that Jefferson's comments "may be accepted almost as an authoritative declaration of the scope and effect of the (First) Amendment." In *Everson v. Board of Education* (1947), Justice Hugo Black wrote: "In the words of Thomas Jefferson, the clause against establishment of religion by law was intended to erect a wall of separation between church and state."

In 592 Pope Gregory I accepted the role of the bishop of Rome as a temporal ruler of the city. Over time the popes gradually came to rule a large portion of the Italian peninsula from an area near Rome known as the Vatican. (The popes moved their residence to Avignon in France from 1309-1377). In 1879 the various areas (states) were united and the status of the pope was referred to as the "Roman Question." This situation was finally resolved in 1929 by the Lateran Treaty agreed to by King Victor Emmanuel III of Italy and Pope Pius XI.

The agreements included a political treaty which created the state of the Vatican City and guaranteed independent sovereignty to the Holy See. The pope was pledged to perpetual neutrality in international relations and to abstention from mediation in a controversy unless specifically requested by all parties.

The constitution of the Italian Republic adopted in 1947 states that relations between the state and the Catholic Church are regulated by the "Lateran Treaties." This confirmed the first major separation of church and state in a country ruled for over a thousand years by a church.

There are many other examples where the influence of religion in government was changed. One such example is the French Revolution of 1789 and the document known as the Concordant, signed with Rome in 1781, which in effect separated church and state. Catholicism was henceforth to be recognized only as "the religion of the vast majority of French citizens." The Concordant's most dramatic step, however, was to bring the church under the authority of the state which left it with no influence in the government.

In 1998, a Hindu nationalistic political party, the Bharatiya Janata Party (BJP) controlled the government of India. The linkage of religion, the national government, and nationalism led to a degeneration of the separation of church and state in India and a decrease in the level of religious tolerance. An escalation of anti-Christian violence was one manifestation of this linkage. With the subsequent change in government, the level of violence diminished, and India became once more a country of relative religious tolerance and peace.

7

Religious Texts—An Overview

THE BIBLE IS A CANONICAL collection of texts considered sacred in Judaism as well as in Christianity. There is no single "bible." Many bibles exist with varying contents. The term bible is shared between Judaism and Christianity, although the contents of each of their collections of canonical text is not the same. Different religious groups include different books within their canons, in different orders, and sometimes divide or combine books or incorporate additional material into canonical books.

The original writings from the apostles themselves (the autographs) no longer exist. This is due partly to the perishable material (papyrus) used by the writers, and partly to the fact that the Roman emperors decreed the destruction of the sacred books (Edict of Diocletian AD 303).

In 315 AD Athanasius, the bishop of Alexandria, identified the 27 books of the new testament which are today recognized as the Canon of Scripture. In 382-383 Jerome revised the Latin New Testament text in accordance with some Greek manuscripts. Between 390 and 406 he translated the Old Testament directly from Hebrew, and this completed work is known today as the "Old Latin Vulgate." It was said that St. Jerome gathered from all quarters whatever might prove of use to him in this task by accumulating the best possible copies of the bible and other information.

The Christian bible contains, at minimum, 80 books. The Old Testament contains the 24 books of the Hebrew bible divided into 39 books plus 14 Apocrypha. The second part is the New Testament containing 27 books: The 4 canonical Gospels, Acts of the Apostles, 21 Epistles or letters and the Book of Revelation.

The bible was divided into chapters in the 13th century and into verses in the 16th century and is now usually cited by book, chapter and verse. It is widely considered to be the best-selling book of all time.

The Quran (Koran) literally meaning "the recitation" is the central religious text of Islam, which Muslims believe to be a revelation from God (Allah). It is widely regarded as the finest piece of literature in the Arabic language. Muslims consider the Quran to be the only book that has been protected by God from distortion or corruption. However, some significant textual variations (employing different wordings) and deficiencies in the Arabic script mean the relationship between the text of today's Quran and an original text is unclear. Quranic chapters are called suras and verses are called ayahs.

Muslims believe that the Quran was verbally revealed from God to Muhammad through the angel Gabriel gradually over a period of approximately 23 years, beginning on 22 December 609 AD, when Muhammad was 40, and concluding in 632 AD, the year of his death. Shortly after Muhammad's death the recitations were collected by his companions using written Quranic materials and everything that had been memorized of the Quran. However, the Quran did not exist in book form at the time of Muhammad's death and there is agreement among scholars that Muhammad himself did not write down the revelations.

Islamic tradition relates that Muhammad received his first revelation in the Cave of Hira during one of his isolated retreats to the mountains. Thereafter, he received revelations over a period of 23 years. According to *hadith* and Muslim history, after Muhammad emigrated to Medina and formed an independent Muslim community, he ordered many of his companions to recite the Quran and to learn and teach the laws, which were revealed daily. It is related that some of the Quraish who were taken prisoners at the battle of Badr, regained their freedom after they had taught some of the Muslims the simple writing of the time. Thus a group of Muslims gradually became literate. As it was initially spoken, the Quran was recorded on tablets, bones and the wide, flat ends of date palm fronds. Most suras were in use amongst early Muslims since they are mentioned in numerous sayings by both Sunni and Shia sources.

Orthodox Muslims believe that the Quran is the unchanging Word of God. However, some non-Islamic scholars believe differently. For example, Dr. Gerd R. Puin, a renowned Islamicist at Saarland University, Germany, says it is not one single work that has survived unchanged through the centuries. Based on his analysis of Sana's manuscripts, Puin claims that the Quran contains stories that were written before Prophet Mohammed began his ministry and which have subsequently been rewritten. His findings were controversial—and offensive enough to Muslims that the authorities who hold the manuscripts denied Puin further access to them.

Most religious historians view Islam as having been founded in 622 AD. However, many of the followers of Islam believe that Islam existed before Muhammad was born and that the origins of Islam date back to the creation of the world.

Hinduism differs from Christianity and other monotheistic religions in that it does not have:

- a single founder,
- a specific theological system,
- a single concept of deity,
- a single holy text,
- a single system of morality,
- a central religious authority,
- the concept of a prophet.

Hinduism is not a religion in the same sense as Christianity is; it is more like an all-encompassing way of life—much as Native American spirituality is.

Hinduism is generally regarded as the world's oldest organized religion. It consists of thousands of different religious groups that have evolved in India since 1500 BCE. Because of the wide variety of Hindu traditions, freedom of belief and practice are notable features of Hinduism.

Most forms of Hinduism are henotheistic religions. They recognize a single deity and view other Gods and Goddesses as manifestations or aspects of that supreme God. Henotheistic and polytheistic religions have traditionally been among the world's most religiously tolerant faiths. As a result, India has traditionally been one of the most religiously tolerant in the world.

Hinduism has grown to become the world's third largest religion, after Christianity and Islam. It claims about 950 million followers—about 14% of the world's population. It is the dominant religion in India, Nepal and among the Tamils in Sri Lanka.

8

Religious Beliefs—Christian, Islam, Hindu

CHRISTIANITY AND ISLAM ARE SOMEWHAT related in that they both revere Abraham and certain other patriarchs mentioned in the Hebrew Scriptures. Thus, they are sometimes called Abrahamic religions. Although there are points of similarity between Christianity and Islam, it is important to understand that there are many differences making it impossible to precisely compare and contrast the two.

Christianity consists of many different religions and Islam is divided into many different traditions including Sunni, Shiite and Sufi to further complicate comparisons.

All mainstream religions have some things in common, for example:

Buddhism—Consider others as ourselves.

Christian—Do unto others as you would have done unto you.

Confucius—What you do not want done to yourself, do not do unto others.

Hindu—No man do to another that which would be repugnant to himself.

Judaism—Thou shalt love they neighbor as myself.

Islam—Not one of you is a believer until he loves for his brother what he loves for himself.

God (Allah) be with us has been the war cry of both sides of virtually every war from the beginning of organized religion.

To complicate matters further, religious practices and beliefs throughout the world are influenced by many factors:

- What the religion's holy book says
- How passages in the book is interpreted by theologians and clergy
- The impact of scientific findings
- The culture in which the religion is embedded

These factors vary from country to country and lead to selective reading of the holy books to find justification for local practices.

Beliefs:

Name of the religion:	Christianity	Islam
Concept of deity:	Most believe in the Trinity; three persons in a single Godhead: Father, Son and Holy Spirit	God (Allah) is one and indivisible. They believe in a strict monotheism. *"Allah"* means God in Arabic.
Status of Yeshua of Nazareth (Jesus Christ):	Generally considered the Son of God; worshiped as God; one person of the Trinity.	Very highly respected as the second-last prophet; second only to Muhammad in importance.
Conception/birth of Yeshua:	Conservatives: virgin conception. Liberals: conventional birth.	Virgin conception.
Death of Yeshua:	Authorized by Pontius Pilate and executed by Roman Army circa 30 CE by crucifixion.	He was neither killed, nor suffered death. Muslims believe that he ascended alive into heaven.

Yeshua's location	Ascended into Heaven	Ascended into Heaven
Identity of "another helper" or "comforter" *	Holy Spirit	Muhammad
Second coming of Jesus	Conservatives: expect in near future. Liberals: varied beliefs.	Anticipate his second coming in the future.
Status of Adam:	Disobeyed God in the Garden of Eden. With Eve, is responsible for original sin that affects all of their descendents down to all persons alive today.	As with Christianity, Adam is believed to have been tempted by Satan and disobeyed God. However, God forgave him for his sins. Muslims have no concept of original sin. Adam is considered a prophet.
Main holy book:	Bible, consisting of Hebrew Scriptures and Christian Scriptures	Qur'an
Original languages:	Hebrew, Aramaic, Greek.	Arabic.
Status of the holy book:	Conservatives: the inerrant Word of God. Liberals: a historical document.	God's word and final revelation, dictated by angel Gabriel to Muhammad. He passed it on in oral form. A slightly imperfect copy of a perfect copy in Paradise.
Additional guidance:	Writings of the leaders of the early Church. For Roman Catholics: church tradition.	The Hadith— sayings and stories of Muhammad (pbuh), his companions and relatives.

Ethic of reciprocity (Golden rule):	*"Therefore all things whatsoever ye would that men should do to you, do ye even so to them."* Matthew 7:12	*"Not one of you is a believer until he loves for his brother what he loves for himself."* Fourth Hadith of an-Nawawi
A baby's status at birth	Various views. One common view is that a baby is born with a sin nature, separated from God.	All babies are a born in a pure state of submission to Allah. However, as they mature they are often taught other beliefs.
Life after death:	Either Heaven or Hell. Catholics believe in Purgatory as a third, temporary, state.	Paradise or Hell.
Basis of determining who goes to Heaven or Paradise:	There is no consensus in Christianity. Different faith groups hold Various diverse beliefs: e.g. some combination of: repentance, trusting Jesus as Lord and Savior, good works, church sacraments, baptism, avoiding the undefined unforgivable sin, etc.	Once they reach puberty, his/her account of deeds is opened in Paradise. To attain paradise, at death, their good deeds (helping others, testifying to the truth of God, leading a virtuous life) . . . must outweigh their evil deeds.
Confessing sins:	Roman Catholic: to God or Jesus, either directly or through a priest; Others: to God or Jesus	To Allah
Probably the most misunderstood term:	*Immaculate Conception*: Roman Catholics believe that the conception of the Virgin Mary, circa 20 BCE, was without sin. Many incorrectly relate it to Yeshua's conception.	*Jihad:* internal, personal struggle towards the attainment of a noble goal. Many incorrectly equate it to *"holy war."*

The most disturbing belief among radical Muslims, but not found in Islamic writings, is that by their actions (become religious martyrs) they can obtain 50 virgins or the expectation that they will be allowed to choose 70 friends and family members to join them in heaven.

Nine Beliefs of Hinduism

Our beliefs determine our thoughts and attitudes about life, which in turn direct our actions. By our actions, we create our destiny. Beliefs about sacred matters—God, soul and cosmos—are essential to one's approach to life. Hindus believe many diverse things, but there are a few bedrock concepts on which most Hindus concur. The following nine beliefs, though not exhaustive, offer a simple summary of Hindu spirituality.

1. Hindus believe in a one, all-pervasive Supreme Being who is both immanent and transcendent, both Creator and Unmanifest Reality.
2. Hindus believe in the divinity of the four Vedas, the world's most ancient scripture, and venerate the Agamas as equally revealed. These primordial hymns are God's word and the bedrock of Sanatana Dharma, the eternal religion.
3. Hindus believe that the universe undergoes endless cycles of creation, preservation and dissolution.
4. Hindus believe in karma, the law of cause and effect by which each individual creates his own destiny by his thoughts, words and deeds.
5. Hindus believe that the soul reincarnates, evolving through many births until all karmas have been resolved, and moksha, liberation from the cycle of rebirth, is attained. Not a single soul will be deprived of this destiny.

6. Hindus believe that divine beings exist in unseen worlds and that temple worship, rituals, sacraments and personal devotionals create a communion with these devas and Gods.
7. Hindus believe that an enlightened master, or satguru, is essential to know the Transcendent Absolute, as are personal discipline, good conduct, purification, pilgrimage, self-inquiry, meditation and surrender in God.
8. Hindus believe that all life is sacred, to be loved and revered, and therefore practice ahimsa, noninjury, in thought, word and deed.
9. Hindus believe that no religion teaches the only way to salvation above all others, but that all genuine paths are facets of God's Light, deserving tolerance and understanding.

Hinduism, the world's oldest religion, has no beginning— it precedes recorded history. It has no human founder. It is a mystical religion, leading the devotee to personally experience the Truth within, finally reaching the pinnacle of consciousness where man and God are one. Hinduism has four main denominations—Saivism, Shaktism, Vaishnavism and Smartism.

Buddhism was introduced to China 2000 years ago and is widely accepted today by most Chinese people. Buddhism in China consists of three sections – Han, Tibetan and southern Buddhism. Many other religions have been brought into the country (Christian faiths and Islam) but none has developed much appeal. Almost 85% of the Chinese have religious beliefs and about 15% are considered atheists.

Confucian is often associated with China but it actually has worldwide influence. Confucianism is not a real religion, it is an ethical and philosophical system developed from Confucius' thoughts.

The Japanese identify their religious beliefs as Shinto or Japanese Buddhism with a small number as Christians. Religion does not play an important role in the everyday life of most people today. Many Japanese participate in rituals and customs and visit Shinto shrines or Buddhist temples only on special occasions. Although Japan enjoys full religious freedom, it is estimated that 70% to 80% do not consider themselves believers in any religion. A 2001 study found that 65% do not believe in God and 55% do not believe in Buddha.

Russia adopted Christianity in 988 and in 1448 split from the Greek Church and became the Russian Orthodox Church. Land decrees of 1917 and 1918 suppressed religion, caused many years of hard times, and most of the church's land was taken by the government. Under the soviet regime, monks were evicted from their monasteries and the buildings destroyed. It wasn't until the late 1980's and 1990 that laws were passed on the freedom of religion. A 1997 law named Orthodox Christianity to be part of Russia's "historical heritage."

Today Russia is 85% Orthodox Christian. Islam is professed by 5%, with Catholic, protestant and other denominations claiming about 1%. It is estimated that over 50% of the population never attends church services and up to 10% are considered atheist.

9

RELIGIOUS (HOLY) WAR—
CHRISTIAN VS MUSLIM VS MUSLIM

WARS CAUSED BY RELIGIOUS DIFFERENCES are religious wars, not holy wars, as there is nothing holy about them. Wars among Christians during the middle ages killed almost 1/3 of the populations of Europe and were not settled until the peace of Westphalia in 1648. (Further fighting between Christians and Muslims in Europe continued into the 1680's). Likewise, conflicts between Catholics and non-Catholics, such as those in Northern Ireland, cannot be considered religious or holy.

Christians and Muslims have been fighting for 1500 years and most conflicts cannot be considered holy. The Islamic invasions of the Iberian Peninsula (Spain) and of Gaul (France) by Moors, Berbers and Arabs between 711 and 788 introduced the Sharia Rule of Law. Christians did not regain control of these lands until the fall of Granada in 1492 by the armies of Castile and Aragon.

A battle between Christians and Muslims in 636 ended in the killing of over 70,000 Christians. In a battle in 1099 Christians killed some 70,000 Muslims and Jews.

The First Crusade (1096-1099), by Catholics from Europe, to regain control of the Holy Lands began after 461 years of Muslim control. The main objective was the city of Jerusalem but included reclaiming Palestine and Syria. Over the next 200 years 8 more crusades were undertaken, most of them consisting of 30-35,000 men. Thousands of people, including women and children were massacred by both sides. The last crusade ended in 1291 with the Mamluk Dynasty in Egypt defeating the European's coastal stronghold of Acre and driving them out of Palestine.

Today we read of continued fighting between Israel and Palestine, and the savage wars by Islamic radicals in Africa and especially in Sudan. The Taliban, an Islamic fundamentalist political movement in Afghanistan, the majority of which are Pashtun tribesmen, are alleged to be supported by Pakistan and Al-Qaeda imported fighters and provided financial support by Saudi Arabia. The Taliban have been condemned internationally for the massacres committed against Afghan civilians and the brutal treatment of women.

Islamic militants set fire to a locked dormitory at a school in northern Nigeria, then shot and slit the throats of students who tried to escape through windows during a predawn attack March of 2014. At least 58 students were killed, including many who were burned alive. They "slaughtered them like sheep" with machetes, and gunned down those who ran away, said one teacher, Adamu Garba.

Today the greatest threat to world peace is Islamic terrorism. It is a form of religious war committed by Muslims to achieve varying political ends in the name of Allah. They use suicide attacks, a complex rewording of the concept of martyrdom, to accomplish strategic objectives against the free world. They believe that "pure Islam" is only through a literal and strict interpretation of the Quran and Hadith.

Terrorist attacks have occurred all over the world: Africa, Australia, North and South America and throughout Europe and Asia, especially in the Caucasus region. According to "Open Doors USA" the top ten countries persecuting Christians today are: North Korea, Somalia, Syria, Iraq, Afghanistan, Saudi Arabia, Maldives, Pakistan, Iran and Yemen. All these countries are Islamic states with mainly Muslim populations except North Korea which is a dictatorship. It has been estimated that Muslim terrorists have killed over 25,000 people since the 9/11 attacks.

Not only are Muslims fighting and killing non-Muslims around the world, they are killing each other. In Iraq, Sunni and Shiite Muslims are constantly at war, bombing each other's holy sites and killing innocent citizens. There are a number of differences between the two sects but they all stem from who they claim to be the true successor of the Prophet. The Prophet, who claimed to have received messages from God over a 23-year period, preached mainly to his family, and never wrote down a single word or indicated who might succeed him. (It is probable that he and his entire family were illiterate).

Today it is estimated that there are over 1.1 billion Muslims with about 85% Sunnis. It is improbable that the current leaders, Sunni Imams and Shiite Mujtahids, will ever give up their political/religious power or more unlikely agree to settle their different practices and beliefs.

10

Pluralism—The Answer

MERRIAM-WEBSTER DEFINES PLURALISM AS: a situation in which people of different social classes, religions, races, etc., are together in a society but continue to have their different traditions and interests. The belief that people of different social classes, religions, races etc., should live together in a society.

Thomas Jefferson wrote "It is safer to have the whole people respectably enlightened than a few in a high state of science and the many in ignorance." Unfortunately radical Islamists have no idea how to deliver education, services, security, economic growth or peace to their people. If Islamic leaders are unable to convince the radicals that their interpretation of the Quran and Hadith are incorrect, they will never accomplish their goals but remain at the bottom of political and economic power forever.

Madeline Albright, former U.S. Secretary of State, in *"The Mighty and The Almighty"* writes in detail the problems in dealing with governments influenced by religion, or worse, controlled by religious fanatics but suggests an original approach to incorporating religion into international politics.

Former U.S. president Bill Clinton's Global Initiative, the UN Alliance of Civilizations, the Global Forum of Spiritual and Parliamentary Leaders (Oxford 1988), Joint Appeal of Science and Religion (New York 1991), and a number of multi-faith efforts to bring understanding and peace between Christians, Jews and Muslims have resulted in little success.

Regardless of the outcome of previous efforts, continued fighting is not the answer.

I believe the only way to worldwide pluralism is through a massive U.N. effort to educate the radical Islamist that 1500 years of fighting and killing has brought them nothing but disrespect, isolation and poverty. The first step will require an expanded U.N. program to provide the forces and funding necessary to stop radical Muslims attacks everywhere in the world (an example would be the French sending troops to the Sudan), and to then improve the infrastructure in those areas. This could include building roads, schools, medical facilities, electrical power plants, and any other means that could provide security and raise the standard of living.

No single nation can accomplish any of this alone because of the cost and lack of authority to do so. Only a committed U.N. resolution could add credibility to such a task.

The next step would be to bring the leaders of every major religion, especially the Islam sects, together to inform and convince radical Muslims that they are completely out of step with the rest of the world. The Islamic schools (Madrasah and Wahabi), that teach mainly a radical interpretation of the Quran, must be shut down and replaced with schools that teach a world-wide view.

The major religions should work together to develop a non-religion based curriculum that could include world history, the ancient religions/myths, the value of separation of government and religion, the scientific understanding of our place in the universe, the evidence of evolution, the need for pluralism, and maybe the similarities and differences of today's religions, all of which I have touched on briefly in this paper.

Some may argue the cost to be too high and the task too large. The fact is that many countries have already spent more on their own security than a U.N. initiative would cost. In the U.S. we have lost personal freedom (The Patriot Act, NSA, TSA) and spent billions of taxpayer dollars on security and fighting wars (Afghanistan, Iraq, etc.) than it would take to support a U.N. world-wide effort. If such a combined and sustained effort is not undertaken soon, the fighting and terror will continue until large portions of the world will be overrun or dominated by Muslims who will then force their beliefs (Sharia Law) on others. The eventual result will likely be a religious war the likes of which the world has never seen.

REFERENCES

Bible
Billions & Billions—Carl Sagan
Koran (Quran)
National Geographic
Smithsonian
Pale Blue Dot—Carl Sagan
The Indianapolis Star (various news articles)
The Mighty and the Almighty—Madeleine Albright
The New York Times (various news articles)
The Outline of History—H.G. Wells
The Inner Reaches of Outer Space—Joseph Campbell
Time
U.S. News & World Report
Wikipedia, The Free Encyclopedia (various subjects)

ABOUT THE AUTHOR

THE AUTHOR WAS RAISED A Catholic and taught to believe the Catholic Church to be the true church and the pope to be the successor of Christ and thus infallible. While serving in the US Army he used free time to read and study the bible. He came to think of the Old Testament as merely fables. The New Testament seemed believable because historically Christ lived and was crucified.

After his time in the army the next few decades were consumed with raising a family, advancing his career and earning a BA in business management. He made a Cursillo, a very emotional experience, became a lector/commentator at Mass and for a short time taught a religion class for high school students. It was during this time that it occurred to him that the strongest argument against being a non-believer is that you could spend eternity in hell. He realized that many peoples' belief in the church and God were based on fear.

His work required travel to 65 countries which gave him the opportunity to meet many interesting and highly educated people. The interaction with people and learning of their history and religion was enlightening.

After much research he came to the belief that the major cause of trouble around the world is conflict between Christians and Muslims and we must find a way to end the killing and bring peace and security to the world.